12 Years a Slave

Solomon Northup

LEVEL 3

SCHOLASTIC

Adapted by: Jane Rollason

Publisher: Jacquie Bloese

Editor: Sarah Silver

Designer: Sarah Peden

Picture research: Pupak Navabpour

Photo credits:
Page 5: Stock Montage/Getty Images.
Pages 6-7: Archive Photos/Getty Images; North Wind Pictures/Alamy.
Pages 58-59: National Geographic/Alamy; Heritage Images, Hulton Archive/Getty Images; The Granger Collection/TopFoto.

Published by Scholastic Ltd 2014

Mary Glasgow Magazines (Scholastic Ltd.)
Euston House
24 Eversholt Street
London NW1 1DB

Printed in Malaysia

Reprinted in 2015

Contents

PEOPLE AND PLACES

SOLOMON NORTHUP
is a free man who becomes a slave. He tells this story.

ANNE NORTHUP
is Solomon's wife.

MR HENRY NORTHUP
is a friend of Solomon and his family.

JAMES H. BURCH
buys and sells slaves in Washington, DC.

MERRILL BROWN and **ABRAM HAMILTON**
meet Solomon in Saratoga and tell him they work in a circus.

WILLIAM FORD
is a plantation owner in Louisiana.

PATSEY
is a slave on the Epps plantation.

ELIZA
is a slave with two children, Randall and Emily.

BASS
is a Canadian who builds houses in Louisiana.

EDWIN EPPS
is a plantation owner in Louisiana.

JOHN M. TIBEATS
does building work for plantation owners.

PLACES Solomon's journey through the United States

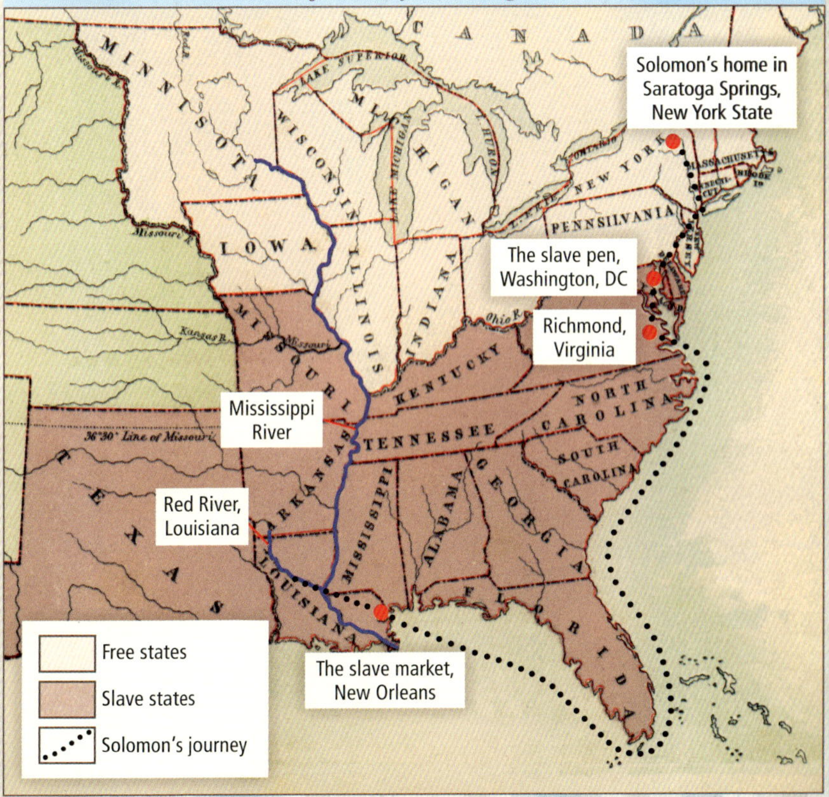

Slavery in the

1619

Ten black slaves arrive to work on a cotton plantation in Virginia, on the south coast of North America. They are the first black slaves in North America.

1619-1808

Of the 12.5 million slaves taken to the Americas from Africa, 388,000 are sold to white people in the United States. Most of the rest go to Brazil and the Caribbean.

1600 1700

The language of the plantation

Many slaves worked on cotton and sugar **plantations** in the South. Each plantation had an owner, called the **planter**. The planter bought his slaves from a slave **dealer** at a slave market. He usually employed an **overseer** to watch the slaves at work.

The overseer rode a horse through the fields and carried a whip. In each group of slaves there was a **driver**. As well as doing a day's work, the driver had to watch the other slaves, and whip any slave who was too slow.

A slave was not allowed to speak to a white person, except to answer a question. When the slave spoke to a plantation owner, he or she called them **Master** or **Mistress**. Planters usually addressed a slave as **Boy** or **Girl**.

United States

1791

People need cotton to make clothes and many other things. A new machine for making cotton is designed. It can make cotton more quickly. Cotton becomes very valuable and plantation owners suddenly need many more cheap workers. There is a big market for slaves.

1800 1900

1808

A new law says Americans cannot bring slaves from Africa into the United States. However white men can still own black slaves in some states, including Louisiana.

1841

Solomon Northup's story begins.

1853

Solomon's story ends.

1860

A government study shows that there are 4.4 million African Americans in the United States. Only ten per cent of them are free.

1861

The American Civil War begins. The South fights against the North. The South wants to keep slavery.

1863

Abraham Lincoln, the President of the United States, passes a law that says 'all slaves are free now and in the future'.

1865

The North wins the Civil War but President Lincoln is shot dead. The United States passes the 13th Amendment. It says that slavery is against the law everywhere in the United States.

12 Years a Slave

Chapter 1
Home

I have a story to tell about a slave. It is my own story and I was the slave. This is a true record of the facts.

My name is Solomon Northup and I was born a free man. I lived a free life in a free state in the North of America for more than thirty years.

My father was not born free. He was a slave, and he belonged to a white man named Mr Northup. The Northups were a good family, and when old Mr Northup died, my father became a free man. He took the name Mintus Northup and the Northup family continued to take an interest in him and his children.

My father married and had two sons. I was the second son, born in July 1808. Our family moved around as my father found jobs on different farms. He was a hard worker and everyone said he was an honest man. He earned enough money to send my brother and me to school.

As a teenager, I worked in the fields with my father. In my free time, I read books or played the violin, which I loved. Music has often helped me through dark times in my life.

My father died in 1829. That same year, on Christmas Day, I married Anne Hampton, a girl who lived near us. She could read and write, and was an excellent cook.

I was twenty-one, with no father to guide me and a new wife at my side. I dreamt of owning a house and land, and I decided to work very hard to get it. I worked building the Champlain Canal, which opened in the spring of 1830. I was well paid, and was able to buy two horses and some equipment. I started a business moving timber from Lake Champlain along the canals and rivers. I employed several men to help me and we built rafts to move the wood. On one trip, I visited Montreal in Canada.

Three years later, Anne and I moved to a farm in a town called Kingsbury. We bought a few animals and planted vegetables. Anne worked in the house and I worked on the land. During the winter, I often played the violin at dances and Anne was sometimes employed as a cook for two or three weeks at a time at Sherrill's Coffee House. Soon we had three wonderful children – Elizabeth, Margaret and Alonzo.

With our land, my music and Anne's cooking, we lived a simple but comfortable life. We thought we could improve our lives, however, and in March 1834 we moved to Saratoga Springs. It was a place that city people visited for their holidays. Anne and I both worked at the United States Hotel in the summer, when visitors came. In the winter, I played the violin and worked on the new railway line to Saratoga.

While we were working at the United States Hotel, I often met slaves who were travelling with their masters from the South. Although their lives were comfortable, they all wanted to be free. But they didn't try to escape, because the punishment for runaways was awful.

At that time, I didn't understand what they were afraid of. Until you have lived as a slave, you can have no idea what a terrible life it is. I had always enjoyed the free air of the North, and my hopes and feelings were no different from those of a white man.

So far my history is ordinary. I was making my way quietly through the world, like any working man. I did not see the clouds that were coming towards me.

Chapter 2
Two strangers

One spring day, in 1841, I was looking for work. Anne was twenty miles* away, working as the cook at Sherrill's Coffee House for a few weeks. She had taken our daughter Elizabeth with her. Margaret and Alonzo were staying with their aunt.

I was walking around Saratoga, when two strangers stopped me. They were well-dressed white men, and they

* 1 mile = 1.6 kilometres. Miles are still used instead of kilometres in the United States today.

introduced themselves to me as Merrill Brown and Abram Hamilton.

'We work in a circus, Mr Northup,' Mr Brown explained. 'At the moment our circus is in Washington, waiting to start a summer tour. We're taking a short holiday, and having a look around Saratoga.'

'We'd like to do a few shows on our journey back to Washington, Mr Northup,' said Mr Hamilton. 'A friend of yours has told us about your excellent violin playing. Would you come with us as our musician? Just as far as New York.'

The pay was a dollar a day, plus three dollars for each show.

'I accept your offer, gentlemen,' I said. 'I have never visited New York City, and right now, I need the work.'

We left immediately. Anne was away for two more weeks, so I did not write to her.

We did some shows in small towns and then arrived in New York. I expected to return to Saratoga at this point, but the two men asked me to continue to Washington with them. They said the circus was travelling into the north for the summer, and that I could earn a lot of money. I knew that Washington was in a slave state, but I did not feel in any danger. I was enjoying the adventure and I decided to go with my new friends.

We arrived in the evening and stayed in a hotel on Pennsylvania Avenue. The next day was Sunday, and Hamilton explained that the circus was closed. They took me to see the White House* and other places of interest, staying close to me all day.

* The White House has been the home and office of the President of the United States since 1800.

Several times we stopped for a drink. Each time they poured a glass of wine for themselves and then gave me one. I drank a little, but I was not drunk. Towards evening, however, I began to feel very unwell. My head ached and I could not eat. My friends said they were worried about me and we returned to the hotel. I managed to climb the stairs to my room, and I threw myself on the bed. The pain in my head was getting worse. During the night some people came into my room, but I have no idea who they were. They told me I needed to visit a doctor, and led me outside. That is the last thing I remembered.

When I awoke, my head did not ache so badly. But I found myself in the most terrible place. I was alone in a cold, dark room, and I was tied to the floor.

Chapter 3
The slave pen

For several hours I tried to understand what had happened. I began to hear sounds from the street outside, and I realised it was daytime. Then I heard footsteps, and a key in the lock. The door opened and the room filled with light. A man came in. He was large and strong-looking with an ugly face and cruel eyes. A second man stood behind him, holding a thick piece of wood.

'Well, boy,' said the first man. 'How do you feel now?'

'I'm sick,' I answered. 'Why am I here?'

'I've bought you, boy,' he said. 'You now belong to James Burch, slave dealer. That's me. I'm going to send you to the slave market in New Orleans, where I can sell you for a very good price.'

'Sir, I am a free man,' I said angrily. 'I live in Saratoga, New York State, and I have a wife and three children, who are also free. My name is Solomon Northup. When I am rescued, you will be in trouble. Take these ropes off me now, sir.'

'Be quiet, boy,' said Burch. 'You are a slave, and I own you.'

I refused to be quiet, however, and Burch became very angry. He said I was lying and that I was a runaway from Washington.

The second man now stepped forward and pushed me to the ground. He pulled the shirt off my back and handed the piece of wood to Burch, who began to hit me. He hit me again and again. I cried out in pain. When his arm was tired, he stopped for a moment.

'Are you a free man?' he asked.

'I am no man's slave!' I shouted.

He started to hit me again, this time harder and faster, until the piece of wood broke. Then he asked me the same question, but I refused to change my answer.

'Fetch the whip, Radburn!' he shouted to the other man.

The whip was worse and each lash burnt my back. Finally, after a long time, he stopped.

'If you ever say you are a free man again,' he said through closed teeth, 'I will whip you to death.'

The two men left the room and locked the door, leaving me in the dark.

* * *

Food and water arrived twice a day. When I was asleep, I saw the happy faces of my children in my dreams. When I was awake, I thought about escape.

'Surely Brown and Hamilton will look for me,' I thought.

After a few days, I was allowed out into a yard. There I met other slaves, who explained that we were in a slave pen. They told me their stories. One was a young boy called Randall. Most of the time he played in the yard, but often he cried for his mother.

I was in the slave pen for two weeks. On my last evening, a woman and her little child were brought in. They were Randall's mother and sister, and they were very happy to see him again. The little girl was very pretty. The woman was called Eliza, her clothes were expensive and she spoke well. She held her children close to her as she told me her story.

Eliza was a slave born on the plantation of a rich white man, called Elisha Berry, in Washington. Berry hated his wife, and built a new house for himself on his land. He moved Eliza and Randall in to live with him. The next year, Emily was born. Eliza had a comfortable life there, and Berry promised to make her free. But then he suddenly died. That very day, Mrs Berry sold Eliza and her children to Burch.

'My poor children,' she cried. 'They'll take them away and my heart will break. I will never see them again.'

That night Burch and Radburn opened up the doors. Radburn tied us in a line and Burch told us to start walking. We went out into the dark streets. All was quiet. Nobody saw us as we walked through the centre of Washington. We could see the Capitol – the home of government – where politicians talked of Americans being free and everyone's right to be happy. 'Everyone' did not include black slaves.

Chapter 4
To the South

Our sad group walked through the Washington streets to the Potomac River, where we were pushed onto a boat. Only the children slept that night. The idea of going to the South was terrible to us. We were afraid that we would never see the North again.

From now on, I decided not to say that I was a free man. I didn't want to bring attention to myself while I looked for a chance to escape.

We travelled by river, road and railway, before arriving at a slave pen in Richmond, the capital of Virginia. We were in the South. There, Burch sold us to a man called Goodin, another slave dealer. Goodin looked at us very closely, working out our price.

'Well, boy, where did you come from?' Goodin asked me.

'New York,' I answered, without thinking.

'New York!' he said, surprised. 'What were you doing up there?'

Burch was staring at me. He was angry.

'Oh, I was visiting up there for a short time,' I said quickly.

Goodin then looked at Burch's other slaves. He liked little Emily very much.

'Very good, Burch,' he said. 'They're a very good collection.'

When their business was over, Burch pushed me into a corner.

'I only said I had been to New York, Master Burch,' I said. 'I didn't say I was a free man. I wasn't thinking.'

'If you ever say the words "New York" or "free man" again, I'll kill you,' he said.

He knew it was a crime to sell a free man into slavery. He meant what he said.

The next day Burch returned to Washington, and Goodin put us on a boat to New Orleans. We were on the boat for many days, and it was my job to hand out bread and meat to each slave twice a day.

I became friends with two other slaves. They were free men like me, and their names were Robert and Arthur. Robert had a wife and two children in Cincinnati. Arthur's family was in Norfolk, and he worked as a builder. He had many friends there. The idea of being someone's slave was terrible for us. We made an escape plan.

In the daytime we were free to walk about on deck. At night we were pushed below deck and locked up.

'Let's try hiding during the day,' Arthur said. 'They don't count us when we go below deck for the night. Nobody will notice if we're missing.'

I decided to try it the next evening, so after supper, I hid under a small boat on deck. In the morning, nobody saw me come out and I joined the others for breakfast. It worked.

Robert's job was to take food and drink to the captain's cabin. He learnt where the captain and his men slept. He knew that there were two guns and a large knife on a table by the door.

The next day, I went over the plan with Arthur and Robert for the last time.

'Arthur and I will spend tonight under the small boat. In the middle of the night, we'll enter the captain's cabin and take the guns and knife. Robert will wait below deck with the slaves and we'll let them out. We'll fight the captain's men, and either win or die. Then we'll sail the boat to the North, and we'll be free.'

The plan was good and we were ready.

But we never had a chance to try it. That afternoon, Robert became very ill. It was smallpox* and four days later he died. Everyone on the boat was now afraid of catching smallpox. As we pushed Robert's body off the boat into the water, we felt very low.

We arrived in New Orleans a day later. Two friends of Arthur's had travelled from Norfolk and were waiting for our boat. They had come to rescue him. He jumped up and down, and fell into their arms when we climbed off the boat. I was very happy for Arthur. But I was sad that nobody knew where *I* was.

Goodin's slaves, including me and Eliza, were collected by a man called Theophilus Freeman. He called each person's name in turn. The last name he called was 'Platt'. Nobody came forward.

* Smallpox was a terrible illness that killed millions of people over many centuries; it passed easily from person to person.

'Where's Platt?' he asked the sailors. Nobody knew anyone of that name.

'Who are you?' he asked, pointing at me. 'Are you one of Goodin's?'

'Yes, sir,' I said.

'Then you're Platt,' he said. 'Why don't you answer, boy?'

'I don't know the name "Platt",' I said.

'Then I'll have to teach you,' he said.

* * *

We were now driven to Freeman's slave pen. There were fifty or so of us in the pen. Freeman walked around the pen the next morning, kicking the older men and women to wake them up and using his whip on the younger slaves.

We all had to wash, and the men had to shave. There were cheap suits, hats and shoes for the men, and clean dresses for the women. Freeman was not being kind to us. He was preparing us for the slave market.

Chapter 5
For sale

The customers came to see the new slaves. One old gentleman liked me. He lived in New Orleans and wanted a man to drive him around the city. I knew that I could easily escape from New Orleans on one of the boats going north. I hoped that he would buy me. Freeman pointed out all the good things about me, but my price was too high and there was no sale.

A planter from the town of Baton Rouge bought Randall.

'Please buy me and my little girl too,' cried Eliza. 'I will work harder than any slave has ever worked.'

'I don't need women,' said the man. 'I just want the boy.'

Eliza ran to Randall and kissed him again and again.

'Remember me, son,' said Eliza, and her tears fell on his face like rain. Then the planter took Randall off to Baton Rouge.

'I'll never see him again,' cried Eliza.

'Stop that noise,' said Freeman. 'Or I'll give you something to cry about.'

More customers came. One was a handsome gentleman with a kind face and a smile. He talked kindly to us and asked questions about what we could do.

He then discussed prices with Freeman, and we learnt from their conversation that his name was William Ford. He offered a thousand dollars for me and seven hundred for Eliza. Freeman accepted, and immediately Eliza ran to Emily and held her tightly.

'Please, Master,' she said to Ford. 'This is my child. Please buy her too.'

Freeman stepped forward and hit her hard, telling her to be quiet. She fell to the floor but continued to ask Ford to buy her daughter. Her crying was terrible to hear, and Ford was moved by it. He asked Freeman what Emily's price was.

'I won't sell her,' replied Freeman. 'She's not for sale.'

'But it's cruel to take her from her mother,' said Ford. 'I will pay a fair price.'

'When she is a few years older,' said Freeman, 'she'll be very valuable. Look how beautiful she is now. She's half black and half white, and I'll get five thousand dollars for her.'

Freeman refused to change his mind. Eliza and I were pulled out into the street. We could hear Emily calling her mother. Eliza was beside me. I knew she was dying inside. She never saw either of her children again.

Our new owner, Master William Ford, led us to a riverboat. Soon the boat was moving fast up the Mississippi River, and then up the Red River, through the state of Louisiana.

Because Ford had grown up in the South, he saw things in a Southern way and he believed that one man could own another. But Ford was a kind man and he also believed that he must take good care of his slaves.

We were on the riverboat for three days. A discussion went on in my head for the whole journey. One moment I decided to tell Ford my history. The next moment I decided I couldn't trust him. It wasn't safe because I was a strong, fit man and I had a high price.

'If Master Ford doesn't want to help me,' I said to myself, 'a slave dealer will take me deep into Texas. They will change my name again and nobody will ever hear of me. Escape will be impossible.'

I think now that I was wrong. But I decided then to lock my secret up in my heart. From now on, I was Platt from Washington.

We left the boat at Alexandria and went by train to a place called Lamourie, at the end of the railway. We walked another twelve miles along the Texas Road, on a very hot day. By the river, the land was swampy. Further on, on higher ground away from the river, we came into thick woods, called the Pine Woods, where the trees were huge.

The sun was low in the sky when we arrived at a large house. There were many smaller buildings around the house, and some of these were cabins for the slaves. There were gardens filled with fruit trees and areas of rich, green grass. The place was quiet and lonely. It was the home of the Fords, and it was now my prison.

It was soon dark and we were very tired from the long walk. I lay down in my cabin and thought about escaping back to Saratoga. I realised that it was hopeless. I was fifteen hundred miles from home and my heart was heavy.

Chapter 6
Red River

William Ford was a rich man. As well as his large house in Pine Woods, he had a timber business four miles away, on Indian Creek. He also had a plantation in an area called Bayou Boeuf, about thirty miles away.

On our first day, I was sent to Indian Creek with a group of Ford's slaves. They all spoke kindly of Ford, as children speak of their own father. When I told them I came from Washington I had to answer all kinds of questions about the city.

All summer I worked at the timber business. Our job there was to cut down trees and make piles of wood.

Because Ford was good to us, we wanted to please him and we worked hard. He did not whip us, he thanked us.

Life was not so kind to Eliza. Poor Eliza could not forget her children, and Mistress Ford soon became tired of her crying day and night. So Eliza was sent to work on the plantation at Bayou Boeuf.

We had to move the timber from Indian Creek to Lamourie. It went by land, which was difficult and expensive. In my own timber business, I had moved timber by canal. There were no canals here, but there were big areas of water all joined together by narrow rivers. In some places, trees had grown up in the rivers. I worked out a way of moving the timber along the rivers and took my plan to Ford. He liked it and said I could try it.

First we cut down some of the trees in the narrowest parts of the river. Then we built rafts. We piled the wood up on the rafts and started the journey to Lamourie. It took less time than I had expected, and everyone was surprised when the wood arrived safely at Lamourie. People called me 'the cleverest slave in the Pine Woods'.

In the autumn, a white man came to do building work on the Fords' house. His name was John M. Tibeats, and I became his assistant. Tibeats was the opposite of Ford in every way. He was stupid and cruel. He had no home of his own, but did building work for plantation owners along the Red River. The slaves hated him, and even the white men had a low opinion of him.

That winter, in 1842, there was bad news for Master Ford. Mistress Ford's brother had a plantation near Alexandria, and he had money problems. Ford had to send him a lot of money to save his business. He also had to pay Tibeats for nearly a year's work.

So Ford had to sell eighteen slaves, including me. Seventeen of the slaves went to work on a neighbour's plantation. Because I knew how to work with wood, I was sold to Tibeats. I was a valuable slave, however, and Ford continued to own half of me, worth about $400.

That $400 saved my life.

Chapter 7
The fight

Our first building job was on Ford's plantation in Bayou Boeuf. I met Eliza there. I had not seen her for several months, and in that time she had become weak and thin. She asked me many times if I remembered her handsome son and beautiful daughter.

Master Ford's overseer on his plantation was called Mr Chapin. He was a rough man, but he was kind, and he was not a friend of Tibeats.

We were building a kitchen house. From first light until late at night, Tibeats did not allow me a moment's rest. Although I worked hard for him and earned him lots of money, he hated me.

One night, I worked until it was too dark to see. Tibeats gave me my orders for the next day.

'Get up before daylight and fetch a bag of nails from Overseer Chapin,' he said. 'Get back here to the kitchen house, and start putting up the east wall.'

The next morning, Chapin gave me the nails.

'If they're the wrong size,' Chapin said, 'I'll get you some different ones. But start the job with these.'

Chapin then climbed on his horse and rode off to the cotton fields. I got to work on the kitchen house. There was nobody else around.

Tibeats appeared a little later. He seemed angrier than usual.

'I thought I told you to build the east wall,' he said.

'Yes, Master, that's what I'm doing.'

'I told you to get a bag of nails from Chapin,' he said.

'Yes, Master, I did.'

'You got the wrong size,' he said.

He kicked the wall hard and turned to me angrily.

'So you think you're the cleverest slave in the Pine Woods?' he shouted and went to the overseer's house. He came back with a whip.

At first I was frightened and I wanted to run. But I knew I had done nothing wrong. Then I became angry, and before he reached me, I had decided to fight.

'Take off your shirt,' he said.

'Master Tibeats,' I said, looking straight at him, 'I will not take off my shirt.'

He prepared to lash me with the whip. I jumped forward and caught his coat in one hand and his leg in the other. I was much stronger than him and I held him upside down by his leg. Only his head and shoulders touched the ground and I put my foot on his neck. He tried to fight back and I hit him hard.

'I'll pull your heart out!' he shouted. 'You'll die for this.'

I hit him again and again. He screamed for help.

I stopped for a moment and looked around me. Mrs Chapin was watching me through the window. Rachel, a slave woman, was watching from the door. Their mouths were wide open.

Tibeats' screams brought Chapin from the fields. As he rode towards us, I pushed Tibeats away from me. He stood up and brushed his clothes. His face was white but he did not say a word.

'What's happening here?' cried Chapin, jumping from his horse.

'Master Tibeats wants to whip me for using those nails,' I said.

'What's wrong with the nails?' he asked Tibeats.

'They were too large,' said Tibeats, not taking his cruel eyes off me.

'I'm the overseer here,' said Chapin. 'I told Platt to use those nails. It's not his fault.'

'This isn't over,' said Tibeats angrily. After a discussion with Chapin out of my hearing, Tibeats rode away on his horse. Chapin then talked to Rachel for some minutes before coming to talk to me.

'Stay where you are,' he said. 'Don't try to leave the plantation. Tibeats is a bad man, and there'll be trouble before night.'

An hour later, Tibeats returned with two white men. They carried a large whip and a rope. Chapin watched from in front of his house. Then he disappeared inside.

The men tied my hands and feet, and put the rope around my neck.

'Let's hang him from there,' said Tibeats, pointing to a tree.

They started pulling me along the ground.

Chapter 8
On the run

Tibeats and the two men threw the rope over the tree. This is the end, I thought. I imagined the faces of my beautiful children and tears ran down my face. The men pulled the rope until my feet were just touching the ground.

'Stop!' shouted Overseer Chapin. He had come out of his house with a gun in each hand. Tibeats and his men stopped.

'Gentlemen,' said Chapin, when he reached us. 'If you pull that rope any tighter, I will shoot you. I have never seen a slave work harder than Platt. Tibeats, I have wanted to whip you myself many times. Master Ford owns half of that slave. If you kill him, you will have to pay $400 to Master Ford. And you have no right to kill him. There is a law for the slave as well as the white man.'

Chapin then ordered Tibeats' two friends to leave. They jumped on their horses and rode away. Without a word, Tibeats followed them. Chapin immediately sent a slave to the Pine Woods to collect Master Ford.

I stayed where I was, with the rope tight around my neck. My hands and feet were tied, and I couldn't move. The sun climbed in the sky, and the day became hotter and hotter. I had no coat or hat to protect me and the ropes cut into my neck, wrists and feet.

All day, Chapin walked up and down in front of his house. He seemed to expect Tibeats to return at any moment. I don't know why he didn't help me.

I had nothing to eat all day. Once, Rachel brought me a cup of water before running back to the kitchen. I was in great pain.

As the sun was going down, Ford rode up to the house. He walked straight up to me.

'Poor Platt,' he said. 'I'm sorry to find you like this.'

'Thank God that you've come at last, Master Ford,' I said.

He cut the ropes from my hands and feet and pulled the rope over my head.

I tried to walk but I fell like a drunk man. When it was dark I went to my cabin, where I lay down. Eliza made food and drink for me, while Rachel told the other slaves the whole story.

The next morning I went back to work on the kitchen house. Tibeats rode up during the morning and began to work too. We completed the job, and Tibeats said nothing about what had happened.

* * *

Our next job was out of sight of the house. Again I worked alone with Tibeats. I worked in a state of fear, with one eye on my work and the other on my master.

About three days later, I was nailing up a piece of timber.

'That's not straight,' Tibeats said.

'I think it's about right,' I said.

'Don't lie to me,' he said. 'It's too high on the right.'

'Okay, Master,' I said, and moved it down on the right before nailing it into place.

'Now it's all wrong!' he shouted. He was very angry.

I stood there without speaking. I didn't know what to do. He became crazy, and picked up a metal bar.

'I'm going to cut your head open!' he screamed, running towards me.

It was a moment of life or death. I pulled the bar from his hand and threw it into the trees. I pushed him to the ground and put my hands around his throat. His face began to go black. Tibeats wanted to kill me, but I didn't want to kill him.

I decided to run instead. I jumped over a gate and into a field of sugar, where slaves were working. I hid among them.

About an hour later, several slaves told me to run. Tibeats and his two friends had appeared on horseback, and they had eight or ten dogs with them.

I ran towards the river. Plantation owners do not allow their slaves to learn to swim but luckily for me, I had learnt to swim as a boy. When I reached the water, I jumped in and swam away.

The noise of the dogs became quieter. Tibeats could not follow me now, I knew. But that didn't mean I was safe. The swamps of Bayou Boeuf are home to dangerous wildlife. I had lost my shoes and it was difficult to walk across the swampy land. Dry land wasn't safe either. Any slave in the wrong place without a pass must be a runaway. A white man was allowed to shoot a runaway or take him prisoner.

Which was the greatest danger – dogs, wild animals or white men?

Chapter 9
No escape

At midnight, this wild corner of the Louisiana swamp was noisier than any city. There were millions of living things, all awake and busy. Sleep was impossible and I could not stay there.

I decided to turn north and make my way to the Pine Woods. It was the only safe place for me. I walked for hours and gradually the ground became less swampy. The next morning, I came to the Texas Road and followed it until I came to the Fords' house.

Master Ford hardly knew who I was. My clothes were dirty and torn, and I was covered in cuts. He listened to my story, and then sent me to the kitchen for some food. I went to my old cabin and slept.

I awoke in the afternoon and went out to work in Mistress Ford's garden. It was full of beautiful flowers and fruit trees. Mistress Ford came into the garden and told me to rest. But I preferred to work, and I spent three days tidying the garden. I was so grateful to the Fords for saving me, and I always think of their garden as a happy place in a cruel story.

Ford took me back to Bayou Boeuf, where we found Tibeats. Ford was angry with him.

'If you don't sell him, Tibeats,' said Ford. 'I will take him from you.'

The slaves on the plantation, including Eliza, were very surprised to find me there that evening. They were sure that I was dead.

That was the last time I saw Eliza. I learnt later from other slaves that she became too weak to pick cotton on the Bayou Boeuf plantation. One day, when the slaves came back from the fields, they found her dead. She was free at last.

Tibeats did as Ford had told him. He sold me to a new master, a man called Epps. I was no longer Tibeats' dog, and I was thankful for that.

I had not heard of Mr Edwin Epps. But I know now that he is one of the cruellest men in Bayou Boeuf.

Chapter 10
In the cotton fields

Edwin Epps was a tall man with blue eyes and blond hair. His face was sharp and clever, but he had clearly never been to school. He was often drunk, and then he became crazy.

Epps grew cotton on his plantation and picking cotton was my life for many years. We planted the cotton in March and the picking season began in August. The fields looked very beautiful at that time, as if they were covered with snow. We worked along the lines of cotton, picking as fast as we could. Each of us was expected to pick 200 pounds* each day.

Some pickers were naturally quick with their fingers. My hands were good for working with wood but not for picking cotton. The most I ever picked in one day was 180 pounds. I often broke the cotton plants too while I was picking, which was a terrible crime.

The day started at first light. We had ten minutes at midday to eat a piece of cold meat. When the moon was bright, work continued until midnight. Nobody could stop picking until Epps gave the order.

Each bag of cotton was then weighed. Although we were almost too tired to stand, this was the moment of greatest fear. Epps whipped any slave who had picked too little.

Even then, we couldn't go to bed. We had to feed the animals, cut wood and prepare our supper and lunch for the next day. Finally, we lay down on pieces of wood in cabins with no floor or window. After a few hours' sleep, the whole thing started again.

* One pound = 0.45 kilos.

This was our life during the cotton picking season from late August to January. In February we planted corn, which was grown to feed the animals and slaves.

There was never enough to eat and the food was always the same. On Sundays each slave received three and a half pounds of meat and a small bag of corn. That was our food for the week. There was no tea, coffee, sugar or salt.

Punishments happened daily: twenty-five lashes for breaking a cotton plant, fifty for not picking enough cotton, 100 lashes for sleeping late in the morning, 500 for

running away. And the whip was used all day long on slaves who went too slowly. The screams of slaves were heard from morning until night on Epps' plantation.

After the cotton picking season, Epps often went to shoot wild animals with his friends and always returned drunk. He broke dishes and chairs in the house, before picking up his whip and coming outside. Sometimes he hid behind a cabin and lashed the first black face that walked across the yard.

Sometimes he was drunk and happy, and he wanted

music and dancing. Tibeats had told him about my musical skills, and Epps returned from one visit to New Orleans with a violin.

Often it was the middle of the night when Epps woke us and called us into the big house. I played the violin while the others danced, following Epps' orders. He whipped any slave who did not dance fast enough. We still had to be in the cotton field at first light the next day.

For ten years I worked for that hard and cruel man. For ten years I made him richer. He was known as a 'slave breaker', and he believed that his slaves were no better than his dogs or his horses.

In 1845, Epps bought a new plantation, and he moved there with his wife and family, taking nine slaves. I was one of them. For eight years at the new plantation, those other eight slaves were my only friends. As I write this, they are still there living the same life.

One of them was Patsey, granddaughter of a slave brought to Cuba from Guinea in Africa. She was slim and tall, and could run amazingly fast. She could jump over a high gate and she could ride any horse. But she was most famous for picking cotton with both hands at amazing speed. Most days, she picked 500 pounds. From August to January, she was the queen of the field.

Almost everybody loved Patsey. Although she had a terrible life, she smiled and laughed, she worked hard and was beautiful.

When Patsey was a child, Mistress Epps had loved her. She often gave her milk and biscuits in the big house, and played with her. But then Patsey grew into a beautiful woman, and Master Epps became interested in her. Now Mistress Epps was jealous of the poor girl, and often attacked her with pieces of wood or broken bottles. Patsey was punished for the smallest crime or for no crime, and she had the lines of a thousand lashes on her back.

In her darkest moments, Patsey came to me.

'Kill me, Platt,' she said to me one time. 'Take me to the swamp and throw my body in.'

But of course I could not do it.

Chapter 11

A new escape plan

The only holiday slaves got was at Christmas. Some planters gave their slaves six days off. Epps gave us three. It was the only time in the year we looked forward to. It was a time for food, fun and music.

The planters around Bayou Boeuf always joined together to give one big Christmas dinner. Five hundred slaves came together, and white people came to watch. We washed our clothes and hair, and cleaned our shoes. The women loved to tie their hair up with red scarves.

It was usually warm enough at Christmas to eat in the open air, under the stars. There were different kinds of meat and piles of vegetables. There were biscuits and sweet fruits. Men sat along one side of the table, women on the other. If a girl liked a boy, she tried to sit opposite him.

After the meal came the Christmas dance. For one night only, the slaves could forget their troubles and dance the night away.

I always played the violin at the Christmas dance. My playing became famous around Bayou Boeuf, and I often played at dances and dinners for whites. They paid Epps for my time, and the guests gave me money on the night.

I think my violin saved my life. It introduced me to great people and gave me breaks from my cruel master. It earned me money to buy little things, like a pipe and shoes. It made other people happy, and that made me happy.

* * *

In every group of slaves working in the fields, there was a 'driver'. For most of my time with Epps I was the driver. I had to watch the other slaves while I worked. If one of them was too slow, or fell from the heat, I had to whip them. If I did not whip them, Epps whipped me.

Unless Epps was away, he was always watching us at work. If he saw me use the whip freely, he was happy. I learnt great skill with the whip. When I whipped Patsey, for example, the whip lashed through the air and she screamed loudly. In fact, it never quite touched her. We all became very good actors, and Epps never found out.

* * *

Soon after he bought me, Epps asked me if I could read and write.

'A little, sir,' I said.

'If I ever find you with a book,' he said, 'I will give you a hundred lashes.'

He never asked a word about my past life or where I came from. Mistress Epps often asked me about Washington, however.

'You're different from the others,' she said to me. 'I think you've seen a lot more of the world than you say.'

Every day of my ten years with Epps, I thought about escape. I made many plans to run away, but none of them had any chance of success. White men rode around Bayou Boeuf every night looking for runaways. Every plantation had dogs that were trained to catch slaves. The swamps were difficult to cross and we were hundreds of miles from the safe states of the North. My best hope was to get a letter to my family. It sounds easy, but it was nearly impossible. I had no pen and paper. I could not leave the plantation without a pass from Master Epps. The post office refused to send a letter for a slave without instructions from a planter.

But then I got a chance. Epps was away selling his cotton in New Orleans. Mistress Epps sent me to the nearest town for some shopping, including paper. I stole one piece, and hid it under my bed. I made a pen. One night, I wrote my letter and addressed it to Mr Henry Northup, Sandy Hill, New York State.

I kept that letter under my bed for a long time. But I had no way of getting it to the post office. Until one day, when a white man came to work with the slaves.

Chapter 12
The letter

The white man's name was Armsby. He was a stranger in the area, and a poor kind of a man. He wanted a job as an overseer, but none of the planters liked him. He had to take a job with the slaves. A white man in the fields is an unusual sight on Bayou Boeuf.

I decided to ask him to post my letter and so I became friends with him. He said that at weekends he often went to Marksville, a town about twenty miles away. One night, I went to Armsby's cabin and woke him.

'Armsby,' I said quietly. 'Armsby!'

'What's going on?' he said.

'Armsby,' I said. 'I want you to help me. I have a little money from my violin playing. I'll give it to you if you post a letter for me in Marksville.'

'A letter?' he said, with a horrible smile. 'I can do that, Platt, no problem. It will be our secret.'

'I haven't written it yet,' I lied. 'I'll give it to you in a day or two.'

I didn't trust him and I knew I had already taken a big chance.

Epps watched us working the next day as usual. At lunchtime, Armsby went and sat with him. They talked for a long time, and I was very glad that I had not given Armsby the letter.

That night, Epps came into my cabin. He had a knife in his hand.

'Well, boy,' he said to me, 'I understand I've got a clever black boy who writes letters. I wonder who he is!'

'I don't know anything about that, sir,' I said.

'Didn't you wake up Armsby last night,' he said, 'and ask him to send a letter for you?'

'Armsby?' I said. 'I haven't spoken to him in all my life.'

'Well,' said Epps, 'Armsby says you've got a letter.'

'He's lying, Master,' I said. 'I haven't got a pen or paper. I don't know anybody to write to. You know I always tell the truth. I can see what he wants.'

'What does he want?' asked Epps.

'He wants to be an overseer,' I said. 'But you don't need an overseer. You do it well yourself. You've got good slaves. So he tells you we're all going to run away and that you need an overseer. He's telling you lies.'

Epps thought for a while.

'Platt, I believe you're telling the truth. He thinks I'm stupid. He thinks I can't take care of my own slaves. We'll set the dogs on him, Platt!'

After he left my cabin, I took out my letter and burnt it. I watched my hopes go up in smoke.

Chapter 13
A piece of soap

Mistress Epps was not a bad woman. Her father was an important man in the area and she had been to a good school. She was beautiful and clever herself, and she loved music. She often asked me to play the violin for her. She gave us nice things to eat if her husband was away. She was kind to all of us, except Patsey.

When Epps was away, she often ordered me to whip Patsey. I always refused, saying that it made Master Epps angry. But one time, when the master and mistress were both full of hate, Patsey nearly paid with her life.

It was Sunday, and we were washing our clothes in the river as usual. It was a beautiful day, and the sun lit up the fields. Birds sang in the trees. Patsey wasn't there. Epps called for her loudly but nobody had seen her. She returned two hours later, from the neighbour's house.

The neighbour's name was Shaw and he had a black wife, who was very kind to Patsey.

'Where have you been, girl?' Master Epps asked her.

'Just to see Mistress Shaw,' said Patsey, 'She gave me some soap. Mistress Epps gives the other slaves soap, but she won't give me any.'

'You're lying,' shouted Epps, suddenly becoming jealous and crazy. 'You went to see Master Shaw, didn't you?'

'No, Master,' said Patsey, showing the piece of soap in her hand.

The punishment that followed was terrible. We had to tie Patsey to four pieces of wood. The slaves stood in a group, asking God to help Patsey. Epps gave me the whip. I had to whip the poor girl again and again. I hated Epps with all my heart.

'Harder,' screamed Epps after each lash, 'or you're next!'

Her back was bleeding all over but Epps was still wild and angry. I refused to continue and threw down the whip. He took it himself, and hit her ten times harder than I had.

Mistress Epps was watching and enjoying Patsey's screams. And then Patsey fell silent.

Finally, Epps stopped. I carried Patsey to her cabin and we laid her down. For days, she could hardly move. At night, when we returned from the fields, we cared for her body. Her health returned, but the happy, lovely girl did not. She never laughed again and she hardly spoke. Her heart was broken and she dreamed only of being free.

Chapter 14
Light in the dark

In the summer of 1852, Master Epps decided to build a new house. He employed some white builders and he took me out of the fields to help them.

I worked with a man called Bass. He loved to discuss politics and he always had unusual opinions. None of the white men agreed with Bass, but they seemed to enjoy laughing at his ideas. He had lived in Marksville for four years, so he was well known in the area. He was a kind man with a good heart. I was very lucky to meet him.

Sometimes Epps came to talk to Bass. They often discussed slavery.

'It's wrong to own slaves,' said Bass.

'But I paid for them,' laughed Epps. 'They're mine.'

'The law says you can own them,' said Bass. 'But in the sight of God, there's no difference between a white man and a black man. I can see no difference. The United States says that all men are born free.'

Epps laughed louder. 'Blacks are no different from animals,' he said, 'and animals aren't born free. Blacks are stupid. They don't know anything!'

'That's because they're not allowed to know anything,' continued Bass. 'They don't have books and teachers like you and me. Slavery is wrong.'

I stayed as close to Bass as possible. One day, we were working alone on the house. It was the moment to speak.

'Master Bass, what part of the country are you from?' I asked.

'I was born in Canada,' he said. 'Guess where that is!'

'I know where Canada is,' I said. 'I've been there.'

He laughed. 'I expect everyone in Canada knows you.'

'No, Master Bass, I'm not joking. I've been to Montreal, and New York too.' Then I told him the names of all the villages along the Champlain Canal, where I once had my timber business.

He was surprised. 'Well, you *have* been in Canada. I know all those places you named. What are you doing here?'

'I've kept my history secret here,' I said. 'I'm afraid to speak to you too. But I believe I can trust you.'

He promised not to say a word to Epps. And so I told him everything.

'I'm getting old,' he said after hearing my story. 'I've met many people and travelled thousands of miles, but I've never been so upset by one man's story. I knew that slavery was wrong, but now I understand what it means to each slave. It will be dangerous for me, but I will write a letter for you.'

On August the 15th, 1852, he wrote to Mr Henry Northup. We worked out that we had to wait at least six weeks for an answer.

Ten weeks passed, and no reply came. The building was finished, and it was time for Bass to leave. He saw my sad face on the day he left.

'I promise to return at Christmas, Platt,' he said. 'If there's no news then, we'll try something else.'

I was not optimistic. Perhaps Mr Northup had died. Perhaps the letter was lost. Perhaps Bass was lying to me. The other slaves asked me if I was sick. But I said I was fine and kept my thoughts locked in my heart.

Chapter 15
'*Who* is Solomon Northup?'

The day before Christmas, Bass rode into the yard. Epps met him warmly, and they went into the house together. He came to my cabin early the next day.

'No letter yet, Platt,' he said.

It was like a knife in my heart.

'Please write again, Master Bass,' I said.

'It's no use,' he said. 'I've asked too many times at the Marksville post office already. It's too dangerous.'

'Then I must end my days here,' I said.

'No, Platt. I have two jobs to complete in this area, and I'll be ready to leave by April. I am going to visit Saratoga myself.'

I could hardly believe my ears.

'I'm with you, Platt, in life or death.'

And he left.

A week later, on an unusually cold January morning, we were in the cotton field. Epps had just gone inside. We saw two white men ride up to the house. They got off their horses, but instead of going to the house, they started to walk through the cotton fields towards us.

* * *

I am now going to take my story back some weeks.

Mr Henry Northup received the letter from Bass in early September. He discovered a law that allowed a man to rescue a free man from slavery. He wrote to the Governor of New York, with proof that I was a free man from New York State and that I was wrongly held as a slave. My wife Anne also asked other important men in Saratoga to write letters.

The Governor was very interested in the case. Mr Northup left for Washington on December the 14th. There, Mr Northup received more letters from the government. They were open letters to gentlemen in Louisiana, asking them to help find Solomon Northup. Mr Northup continued his journey to Red River, and took a riverboat to Marksville. He arrived there on January the 1st, 1853.

He found a lawyer in Marksville and showed him the letters. Luckily, the lawyer was a good man, and he agreed to help.

'Where is Solomon Northup?' asked Mr Northup.

The lawyer answered with another question. '*Who* is Solomon Northup?'

I had not used that name since I was sold in New Orleans and in his excellent letter, Bass did not include my slave name. In Louisiana, I was Platt and Platt only. There were hundreds of thousands of slaves in the area. They decided to travel around Bayou Boeuf and ask at each plantation for me. This plan had no chance of success. Once the news was out, Epps could send me away to Texas.

Mr Northup and the lawyer were having lunch and discussing slavery.

'Only one man in Marksville ever speaks out against slavery,' said the lawyer. 'His name is Bass.'

Then the lawyer jumped to his feet.

'That's it!' said the lawyer. 'Your letter was sent on August the 15th. Bass was working somewhere on Bayou Boeuf at that time. He's the man we need.'

They left their lunch and went to look for Bass. Marksville is a small place, and they soon found him. They were just in time. He was stepping onto a riverboat and was about to sail away.

Chapter 16
Two white men

Bass told them everything. He drew a map showing the quickest way to get to Epps' plantation.

Mr Northup and the Marksville Sheriff* left the town at once on horseback, although it was after midnight. They didn't want to give Epps time to hide me away, as news began to travel around the area. They brought an extra horse with them and they rode all night.

* * *

And so my story returns to that cold January morning in the cotton field. Two white men were walking towards us through the cotton field. It was an unusual sight.

'Where's the boy they call Platt?' the Sheriff asked.

'I'm right here, Master,' I said.

I knew all the white planters on Bayou Boeuf, but this man was a stranger.

'Platt, do you know that man?' he asked, pointing to the second gentleman.

'Mr Henry Northup!' I cried. 'Oh, thank God!'

I immediately understood the nature of their business. I started to run towards Mr Northup, but the Sheriff stopped me. He asked me several questions about my life in Saratoga. I answered them all and then pushed past him to shake the hand of my dear friend. I could not say another word. I could not hold back my tears.

'Sol,' said Mr Northup. 'I'm glad to see you.'

The other slaves stood with huge eyes and open mouths. For ten years we had been close together and shared our hard lives, but they had never heard my real name.

* The law officer in American towns is called the Sheriff.

'Throw down that cotton bag,' said Mr Northup. 'Your slave days are over. Come with us to find this man Epps.'

As we walked up to the house, I had lots of questions about my family. Henry told me that my wife and my three children were well, but sadly my mother had died.

We reached the house and Epps came out to meet us. He invited the Sheriff and Mr Northup into the house and sent me to fetch some wood.

When I came back with the wood, they were looking at all the papers.

'Why didn't you tell you me, Platt?' asked Epps.

'I told the slave dealer, Burch, that I was a free man, and he nearly whipped me to death,' I said.

'Who wrote that letter for you?' asked Epps.

'Perhaps I wrote it myself,' I said.

'I know it wasn't you,' he replied angrily. 'I'll find him. I paid good money for you – how am I going to get that back?'

Mistress Epps spoke kindly to me. 'I'm very sorry to lose you, Platt,' she said. I think there were even tears in her eyes.

The slaves were all waiting together in the yard. They called me over, and I told them my story as quickly as I could. They couldn't believe it.

The Sheriff and Mr Northup climbed on their horses and called to me. I said goodbye to my friends. Patsey threw her arms around my neck.

'Oh, Platt,' she cried. 'You're going to be free and we'll never see you again. You've saved me from being whipped so many times. I'm glad for you, but what's going to happen to me?'

There was nothing I could say.

I climbed onto the third horse and we rode away. A few minutes later, Epps raced past us on his horse.

'I'm going to Pine Woods,' he shouted. 'To see William Ford.'

* * *

Our journey home took several days. You can imagine my feelings as I stood outside the house where my family now lived. We were all unable to speak for a long while.

My story is completely true. I have made nothing up. Hundreds of free men and women have been taken and sold into slavery, and at this moment are living terrible lives on plantations in Texas and Louisiana.

Epilogue

Solomon and Henry Northup stopped in Washington on their journey home to Saratoga. They went to see lawyers and law officers, and told them about James Burch's part in Solomon's story.

Burch was brought before the law. However, the law in Washington did not allow a black man to speak out against a white man. Burch said that he had bought Solomon honestly, but he had lost the paperwork. The law officers believed Burch and he was set free.

There was huge interest in Solomon's story when he returned to New York in 1853. Friends helped him to tell his story in the book *12 Years a Slave*, which came out only a few months after his rescue. It became a bestseller.

In October 1854, Brown and Hamilton were brought before the law for selling Solomon into slavery. Their real names were Merrill and Russell. Although Solomon was able to tell his story in New York, there was not enough proof. They were set free.

In 1855, Solomon was living with his daughter Margaret. He travelled around the north-eastern United States, telling his story and talking about slavery.
In 1857, when he was preparing to speak in Canada, he disappeared.

Some people think he was caught again, and sent back to the South. Others say he was too old to be a useful slave by then. So far, there is no record of Solomon Northup after that day.

The end of slavery in the United States

After 1800, the campaign to end slavery started to grow slowly in the North. But the slave owners in the South believed this was an attack on their way of life.

The Underground Railroad

From around 1830, the campaign against slavery was helped by stories from the 'Underground Railroad'. This was the name given to the secret routes that slaves used to escape from the South to the North.

The slaves travelled at night, usually fifteen to thirty kilometres between each safe house. They had to hide during the day. They were helped by people who hated slavery. The journey was hard, especially for women and children. It was dangerous too. There were lots of slave catchers, often with dogs, who chased the slaves.

Uncle Tom's Cabin

In 1852, a white woman called Harriet Beecher Stowe wrote *Uncle Tom's Cabin*. Stowe's book told the story of the terrible lives of slaves with cruel slave owners. Stowe lived at the time in Ohio, across the river from the slave state of Kentucky. She hated slavery and she often helped runaways. Her book was very popular in America, selling 300,000 copies in its first year. It persuaded many Americans that slavery must end.

Books changed people's opinions in the nineteenth century. What changes people's opinions today?

Harriet Beecher Stowe

The Civil War

Abraham Lincoln wanted to end slavery. When he became the 16th President of the United States in 1860, the slave states of the South were very unhappy. They decided to leave the United States, and they formed the Confederate States of America. Lincoln refused to accept the break-up of the country.

Abraham Lincoln

In April 1861, the Confederate army attacked a U.S. army building and took down the American flag. The Civil War had started. It was a long and terrible war that lasted until 1865, and 625,000 men died. Many blacks fought for the Union Armies of the North. In April 1865, the North finally won the war.

Slavery ends

After the Union Army won the Civil War, Lincoln brought in a new law called the 13th Amendment. White people could no longer own black slaves. However, this did not make life much easier for black people. It was another hundred years until Martin Luther King helped to win equal rights for black people.

What do these words mean? You can use a dictionary.

campaign route to persuade flag civil war equal rights

Chapters 1-3

Before you read

You can use your dictionary.

1 Match the definitions with the words.

canal yard whip timber pen raft

a) You travel along this on a boat.
b) This is a simple kind of boat – it is flat and square.
c) Live animals are kept in this at markets and shows.
d) This is an outside area that belongs to a house or other building.
e) You can use these long, narrow pieces of wood to make a boat.
f) Long, thin pieces of leather used to hit a person or animal.

2 Choose the correct word(s).

a) A cruel person is *very kind / unkind*.
b) A runaway is a person who *escapes / can move very fast.*
c) You *lash / burn* a person when you hit them across the back.
d) You get a punishment for doing something *good / bad*.

3 Read about slavery on page 6. Are these sentences true or false?

a) Less than ten per cent of all slaves taken from Africa to the Americas went to the United States.
b) Fewer slaves were needed in the 1800s to grow cotton.
c) In 1860 most African Americans in the United States were free.

After you read

4 Tick two boxes to answer each of these questions.

a) Which of these does Solomon do before he is twenty-one?
☐ go to school ☐ work in the fields ☐ become a slave

b) What reasons does Solomon give for going to New York?
☐ he wants a holiday ☐ he has never been there
☐ he needs a job

c) What does James Burch use to hit Solomon?
☐ a piece of wood ☐ a thick rope ☐ a whip

d) Which of these are true about Eliza?
☐ she has two children ☐ she was born free
☐ she has had a comfortable life

5 What do you think?

a) What happened to Solomon after he fell ill in the hotel?

b) Who can help Solomon?

Chapters 4–8

Before you read

6 Match the definitions with the words.

cabin captain deck nail pass swamp trust

a) A kind of ticket that allows you to travel freely.

b) To believe that a person is honest and will do what they say.

c) A small piece of metal with a sharp point.

d) An area of land that is very wet all year round.

e) The most important person on a ship.

f) The outside floor area of a boat.

g) The room where you sleep on a ship.

After you read

7 Answer these questions.

a) Solomon, Arthur and Robert have a good escape plan. Why doesn't it work?

b) Why does Freeman refuse to sell Emily to Ford?

c) Why does Solomon decide not to tell Ford about his past?

d) Why does Ford have to sell Platt to Tibeats?

8 Put these events in the order they happen.

a) Ford sets Platt free.

b) Platt and Tibeats fight, and Platt wins.

c) Platt runs away into the swamps of Bayou Boeuf.

d) Tibeats prepares to whip Platt.

e) Tibeats says Platt is using the wrong nails.

f) Tibeats ties Platt to a tree.

g) Tibeats tries to kill Platt with a metal bar.

9 What do you think?

a) Why does Tibeats hate Platt so much?

b) How does Platt feel when he is in the swamp?

Chapters 9-13

Before you read

10 Choose the correct word.

a) You use *corn / cotton* to make bread.

b) Plantation owners used millions of slaves to *pick / pick up* cotton.

c) If you are *brave / jealous*, you want something that somebody else has.

11 What do you think?
Solomon is in the middle of the swamp with dangers all around. What will he do next?

After you read

12 Correct the mistakes in these sentences.

a) Tibeats tells Ford that he must sell Platt.

b) Platt is very good at picking cotton.

c) The worst crime on the plantation is sleeping late in the morning.

d) When Epps is drunk, his slaves have to get up and pick cotton in the middle of the night.

e) Patsey is called 'queen of the field' because she can ride a horse.

f) Mistress Epps has always hated Patsey.

13 Answer the questions.

a) Who plays the violin at the Christmas dance?

b) Who realises that Platt isn't an ordinary slave?

c) Who writes a letter on stolen paper with a home-made pen?

d) Who promises to post Platt's letter?

e) Who persuades Epps that Armsby is lying?

f) Who refuses to give Patsey soap?

g) Who has to whip Patsey?

14 What do you think?

a) What is the worst part of the slaves' daily life on the Epps' plantation?

b) Mistress Epps hates Patsey. Why doesn't her husband sell Patsey?

Chapters 14-Epilogue

Before you read

15 Complete this sentence:

A **lawyer** is ...

a) a person who helps you if you are in trouble with the police.

b) a person who decides how long to send a criminal to prison for.

16 This is the last part of Solomon's story. How will his life as a slave come to an end, do you think?

After you read

17 Answer the questions.

a) Why does Platt decide to trust Bass?

b) What does Bass agree to do for Platt?

c) What news arrives at Christmas?

d) Why can't Henry Northup find Solomon immediately when he arrives in Marksville?

e) What is Bass about to do when Henry Northup finds him?

f) Why do Henry Northup and the Marksville Sheriff decide to ride through the night to the Epps plantation?

g) What does Solomon do after he answers the Sheriff's questions correctly?

h) What is Epps angry about when he learns the truth about Solomon?

i) Why doesn't Burch go to prison for selling a free man?

j) When and how did Solomon Northup die?

18 What do you think?

a) Will it be easy for Solomon to return to his old life in the North?

b) What is important in life? Put these in order.

- ☐ having enough food and a safe place to sleep
- ☐ having a family
- ☐ being rich
- ☐ going to school
- ☐ being free

New Words

What do these words mean?

cabin (n) ....

canal (n) ....

captain (n) ....

circus (n) ....

corn (n) ....

cruel (adj) ....

deck (n) ....

drunk (adj) ....

jealous (adj) ....

lash (n & v) ....

lawyer (n) ....

nail (n & v) ....

pass (n) ....

pen (slave pen) (n) ....

pick (v) ....

punish (v) .... punishment (n) ....

raft (n) ....

rope (n) ....

runaway (n) ....

slave (n) .... / slavery (n) ....

swamp (n) .... / swampy (adj) ....

timber (n) ....

trust (v) ....

whip (n & v) ....

yard (n) ....